HARLEYS, POPES, AND INDIAN CHIEFS

UNFINISHED BUSINESS OF THE SIXTIES

HARLEYS, POPES, AND INDIAN CHIEFS

UNFINISHED BUSINESS OF THE SIXTIES

TEXT BY TIM PAULSON WITH FREDRIC WINKOWSKI

PHOTOGRAPHS BY FREDRIC WINKOWSKI

DRY TRANSFER ART BY GENE WHEELER

DESIGN BY JAN MELCHIOR

PAVILION

A Packaged Goods Book

First published in Great Britain in 1994 by
PAVILION BOOKS LIMITED
26 UPPER GROUND, LONDON SE1 9PD

This book was conceived and produced by
Packaged Goods Incorporated
9 Murray Street, New York, NY 10007, USA
A Quarto Company

Text by Tim Paulson with Fredric Winkowski
Colour photographs by Fredric Winkowski
Dry Transfers by Gene Wheeler
Ariel overleaf photographs by Ted J. Tine, Jr.
Additional photos reprinted courtesy of
Jan Melchior pp. 65, 90, 94, 99, 105, 110-111
FPG International pp. 26, 37, 50-51, 96
Endpaper photo by Laurence B. Aiuppy
The Bettman Archive pp. 22-23, 34-35, 62, 74
UPI / Bettman Newsphotos p. 82
Fredric Winkowski pp. 31, 59, 65, 86
pp. 6-7 1931 Indian

Design by Jan Melchior

©1994 by Packaged Goods Incorporated

A CIP catalogue record for this book is available from the British Library

ISBN 1 85793 490 3
Colour Separations by Eray Scan Pte Ltd
Printed and bound in Hong Kong by Sing Cheong Printing Co. Ltd.

This book may be ordered by post direct from the publisher.
Please contact the Marketing Department. But try your bookshop first.

HARLEYS, POPES, AND INDIAN CHIEFS

UNFINISHED BUSINESS OF THE SIXTIES

TEXT BY TIM PAULSON WITH FREDRIC WINKOWSKI

PHOTOGRAPHS BY FREDRIC WINKOWSKI

DRY TRANSFER ART BY GENE WHEELER

DESIGN BY JAN MELCHIOR

PAVILION

A Packaged Goods Book

First published in Great Britain in 1994 by
PAVILION BOOKS LIMITED
26 UPPER GROUND, LONDON SE1 9PD

This book was conceived and produced by
Packaged Goods Incorporated
9 Murray Street, New York, NY 10007, USA
A Quarto Company

Text by Tim Paulson with Fredric Winkowski
Colour photographs by Fredric Winkowski
Dry Transfers by Gene Wheeler
Ariel overleaf photographs by Ted J. Tine, Jr.
Additional photos reprinted courtesy of
Jan Melchior pp. 65, 90, 94, 99, 105, 110-111
FPG International pp. 26, 37, 50-51, 96
Endpaper photo by Laurence B. Aiuppy
The Bettman Archive pp. 22-23, 34-35, 62, 74
UPI / Bettman Newsphotos p. 82
Fredric Winkowski pp. 31, 59, 65, 86
pp. 6-7 1931 Indian

Design by Jan Melchior

©1994 by Packaged Goods Incorporated

A CIP catalogue record for this book is available from the British Library

ISBN 1 85793 490 3
Colour Separations by Eray Scan Pte Ltd
Printed and bound in Hong Kong by Sing Cheong Printing Co. Ltd.

This book may be ordered by post direct from the publisher.
Please contact the Marketing Department. But try your bookshop first.

To Donna, who gave me my first ride on a Harley, and to John, who got me my first bike.

—Tim Paulson

To my father Felix, a master photographer, magician of the darkroom and my inspiration. And to my mother Mary, whose creative and playful spirit has influenced all of my work.

—Fredric Winkowski

Acknowledgments

We gratefully acknowledge the assistance of Greg Wozney, who sent us traveling in the right direction; Bill Eggers, restorer, collector, and information pipeline to the world of bikes; Dennis Dittrich in helping create the text; Everett Davidson, for introducing us to the motorcycles in his living room; Frank Sullivan, trusted wing man on many a mission; Greg Bastic at Bike Journal; Marta Hallett, our kind of publisher; and Erik Winkowski, for his assistance and enthusiasm.

For their help with a thousand things and for their dedicated work in restoring the Ariel in time for its appearance in this book, we would like to thank the crew at Essex Motorsports International Inc. in Chester, Connecticut, and especially Ted J. Tine, Jr., President; Bill Leonard, Vice President; Richie Greaves, for powder coating; William H. Douglass, for assembly, fabrication, and machining; Robert Gorske at Roade Studios for the overall paintwork; Bob Meyers at Cycle Colors for paintwork and striping work on the gas tank; Charles Taylor for assembly and engine rebuild; and Mike Freeman for restoration of gauges.

We'd also like to thank Randy Zorin, professional Indian restorer of Lyndenhurst, Long Island; Kevin Ballentine of New Jersey's Colonial Motorcycle Club; Buzz Kantor, who knows everyone in motorcycling; and "Sonny" et al, at Ghost Motorcycle in Port Washington. Special thanks to Bill Banks and his dad, Robin James, and Dragonfly Motorcycles.

And to the many bike owners, collectors, and enthusiasts who have made this project so enjoyable, we give the "thumbs up" to: Dale Axelrod, Martin C. Moran, Geno Palma, Berland and Jaci Sullivan, Bill Schuyler, Jeffery Slobodian, Randy Forgue, Robert B. Totten, Stanley R. Mahan, Richard Frost, Bill Campbell, Reed Martin, Gregory Waltee, Carmen Muzillo, Jeff Baer, Jim Trotta (The Ice Cream Man from Hell), Danny McGill, Ken Sitterley, Paul Walker, John Bova, David Sarafan, Kevin Cameron, and Herbert Wagner.

CONTENTS

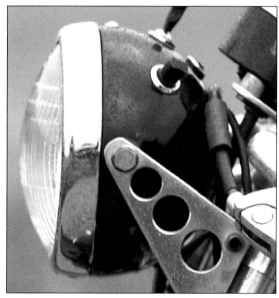

Introduction

This book is dedicated to celebrating the inherent relationships between motorcycles, the individual, and society, through the decades and across the continents. This is neither a catalogue of "great bikes" nor a history of motorcycling, but instead an album of glorious machines—triumphs of both aesthetics and engineering. In its pages the reader can witness the motorcycle's swift and steady evolution as part of the fabric of social history. Within this century alone the motorcycle industry has seen the startling technological leap that began with the De Dion tricycle and culminated with the Japanese "superbikes"; from a one and three-quarter horsepower to four-engine dragsters with over a thousand horsepower.

The motorcycle has always held a unique place in the public consciousness. In the years before World War I, when many automobiles on the road were luxury cars that would cost as much as a house of the times, the motorcycle was an

excellent alternative form of family transport. Coupled with a sidecar, a sturdy bike could haul a maximum of four people —if they had good balance. Henry Ford's Model T changed all that. Suddenly, ordinary people could afford a family car and the character of motorcyclists changed forever. By the thirties, riding a motorcycle generally meant you preferred to get around on two wheels. Bikers had become daredevils.

While motorbikes have been raced from their very inception, probably since the first time two of them were in the same place at the same time, speed records set in the twenties and thirties

were truly shocking. The 123-miles-per-hour set by an Ace Four in 1923 was astounding to people of the time. As technology leaped forward, these records would give the motorcycle an aura of daring speed with which cars could not compete. There was something about the exposed rider, facing the elements with no more protection than a light cotton or leather helmet and sturdy clothing, that set bikers apart. Races organized in 1907 on the Isle of Man in Britain's Irish Sea and the Grand Prix event in France became classic road tests for new models.

When the fifties rolled around, yet another image of the biker would appear on the scene. Starring in the movie, *The Wild One*, Marlon Brando, clad in leather and peaked cap, roared into history as the leader of a biker gang. While he actually rode a Triumph in the movie, Lee Marvin did indeed ride a Harley, and it was Harley-Davidson that was saddled with the negative "biker" image. It's an image they have never tried too hard to shake—although in the sixties and seventies some attempt was made—identifying such malcontents as the Hell's Angels and other gangs such as the "One Percenters," claiming, correctly, that such elements comprised only a tiny fraction of motorcyclists.

The motorcycle's changing place in the American scene has as much to do with how the country has changed through the decades as it does with technology. As the machine age dawned, and America took a bolder, more global view of itself, the very shape of American machines metamorphosed. Gone was the angular, contraption look of the teens and twenties. At the same time, fashions underwent a sea of change. Gone too was the angular, boyish flapper girl. Sleek, streamlined bikes rolled off the assembly lines just as a new, more rounded image of female beauty became the rage. Gas tanks evolved into rounded

bubbles and teardrops, fenders bloomed into statements. Hemlines rose. Austere, Bauhaus buildings gave way to more sumptuous designs. Bikes were draped in leather fringe and saddlebags, fairings stretched their protective wings, and the motorcycle took off into another age. Other symbols of the times lent their style to the motorbike. The long oval of the airship, the matter-of-fact, wind tunnel-tested look of airframes, the smooth fenders of the fifties cars all found echoes in their two-wheeled counterparts. And then, too, after having lived through the events of two world wars America was bent on having fun.

Design

Unlike automobiles, motorcycles needed an honest design from the start. While four-wheeled machines could pretend to be sumptuous carriages with invisible motors, virtually drawing rooms on wheels, it was impossible to conceal the four cylinders of the early Hendersons or Indian V-twins. Nor was concealment perceived as desirable. From the very early days motorcyclists craved noise and power, just as they extolled taking the wind full in the face and feeling the road beneath their wheels. None of that has changed, though. In its continuing metamorphosis, the engine has become cowled and hooded, almost mysterious.

It was during the teens that most bikes shared a common look—a narrow and wiry profile, close to the origins of the bicycle. The parts on these motorcycles seem attached almost temporarily: an engine strapped to a frame, lanterns bolted and guyed to handlebars, fenders strutted and scaffolded. As the twenties approached, a brand new look arrived. Gas tanks began to swell, parts became more integral, and the motorcycle came to be its own entity—no longer just a bicycle with a motor. In terms of design, it was during the thirties that

the motorcycle reached the apex of streamlining, with the addition of Harley-Davidson's teardrop tank. With the skirted fenders of the Indian Roadmaster, a new look ensued, one swathed and cowled to allow the wind to flow smoothly over glossily painted metal and bright chrome. Fairings came into their own in the fifties, as yet more body styling crept into motorcycle design. And yet a British bike from the sixties or even the seventies carries distinctly more than an echo of its counterparts in the thirties. For example, the AJS appears not nearly as dated as a car of virtually any make would from the same

period. To the untutored eye, such a vintage bike might not even look out of place on a modern street. This is testament to the quintessential integrity that is the bedrock of motorcycle design and construction. Natural selection requires this. A motorcycle must stay on the road if it is to stay in production. Mechanical failures in cars are annoying, but in motorcycles they can be fatal. But motorcycles always ensured critical analysis by those who watch them cruise the streets. Somehow the fragility of the structure combined with the speed they attain makes for a curious combination for the bystander.

The Road

Motorcycling is also about the road, and about the shared experience of getting out and "just doing it." Some bikes are for touring—those of 750 ccs or more. Others are cruising bikes, for weekend trips. Still others are sport bikes, meant for getting up to speed on some curvy road somewhere and having a day of it. And, of course, there are the humble commuter motorcycles used by mil-

lions, especially in Asia and Europe.

Harley-Davidson sired a touring lifestyle enjoyed by thousands. There is also a cult of Indian motorcyclists that would defy the understanding of anyone whose heart can resist the shining glory of the 1923 Scout.

With its demise, the Indian company became something almost more powerful than a living company could ever be—a kind of phantom with the power to haunt those who have glimpsed it. Other bikes have developed similar followings. Nortons are praised for their solid construction and raw power; Gileras for the sweet, perfect coupling of low-slung good looks and speed. Ducatis are a

world unto themselves —a world of international racing renown. BMW riders can imagine straddling no other bike. For advocates of the Honda Gold Wing, there is no better way to tour the country than by sliding along swathed in half a ton of technology and comfort. Dirt bikers also have little use for anything but their Suzukis, Kawasakis, and Yamahas.

The motorcycles featured in this book were photographed at numerous meets and shows and each cycle is a treasured piece of art that has been carefully restored and modified by its loving collector. The bikes have been placed chronologically, so the main aspects of their different com-

ponents relate to the year. For example, the Harley-Davidson pictured on page 68, has a 1949

seat, an added windshield, and the saddlebags have been removed—but the chassis is essentially a 1952 Hydra-Glide.

TRICYCLE CRAZE
1898
De Dion-Bouton Tricycle

Tricycles like this one were a phenomenon in the 1890s. Tricycle races were popular sport in Europe, and a unit of the British army was actually equipped with three-wheelers powered by the same one and three-quarter horsepower of this model. It was not until the advent of a lighter, more compactly designed power plant that the now-standard two-wheeler became the natural form for all motorcycles.

The tricycle shown here has a unique history. It was commissioned by Harold Vanderbilt in 1899 to pace bicycle races on the board track at New York's Madison Square Garden. Count de Dion was the money, Georges Bouton was the engineer, and what they produced was the most spectacularly successful motorcycle engine of the late nineteenth century. So successful was it that neither man received much money for their achievement—the design was readily copied by motorbike designers the world over.

Since that time, the machine has enjoyed the vicissitudes of fate so many of these classic bikes have known, falling in and out of restoration. In 1939 it was discovered, dilapidated, in a barn in the eastern United States, only to fall back into ruin a few decades later. It was rescued for a second time in 1991—more than a

century after its construction by producer De Dion-Bouton.

One of the unique aspects of this particular example of the De Dion-Bouton tricycle is its very narrow width—just 32 inches from hub to hub. Narrow enough, in fact, to pass through an average door. It is the only De Dion-

Bouton with this feature, which may have been designed to accommodate the extremely narrow track used in board-track bicycle racing.

Shortly after its restoration, this bike raced as the oldest in the classic London to Brighton run of pre-1905 transportation. The trike does

have a few nonoriginal features—the paint job is not the maroon finish of the Vanderbilt livery, and the oiling system and clutch have been slightly modified to make it safer and more reliable.

This tricycle is still equipped with its original cyclometer. The clutch, attached

to the frame, was capable of disengaging the trike's one gear—an advanced feature for the time. On the open road this vehicle, still used by the owner for the occasional errand, is capable of moving at fifteen miles per hour—no doubt a brisk pace in the 1890s.

1904 Marsh

DELIVERY VAN
1911
Minneapolis
Forecar

The candy-apple red of this attractive three-wheeler evokes an era of straw boaters, good manners, and good times. America had not yet known a world war when it was built. Those pre-war days were the heyday of the motorcycle. Vehicles like this one were used for just about every purpose, being cheaper to buy and to own than automobiles, which at this time were generally produced by the rich for the rich.

This machine is absolutely rare—the only one of its kind still around. In the days before four-wheeled transport became cheap and affordable, motorcycles proliferated in America, with at one time nearly fifty companies competing for riders. Sidecars were popular, but for commercial requirements, the tricycle was ideal. This particular model was used for making deliveries.

The Minneapolis shares the crankstart common on automobiles of this era, as well as a foot-operated clutch and brake. The clutch is actually unitized to the engine, and it has a two-speed transmission. The Minneapolis motor is more than ample to propel the Forecar on its daily missions around town and weekend excursions.

THE SILENT GRAY FELLOW
1913
Harley-Davidson

hen Bill Harley and Arthur Davidson began experimenting with motorized bicycles in 1901, they had no idea about the legend they were kickstarting. What Harley and the Davidson brothers built in a backyard shed in 1903 bears little resemblance to the Harleys seen today, but it did resemble the 1913 model shown here. It is often said that the carburetor on their earliest bike was fabricated from a tomato soup can.

This 1913 bike looks substantially like the 1903 factory prototype, but the differences are significant. The first bike was seen to be

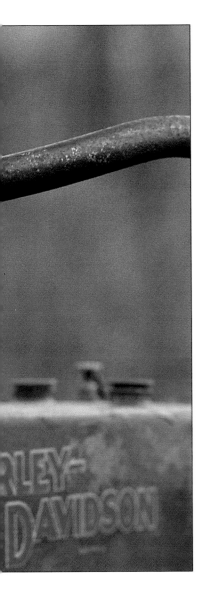

under-powered, which was remedied by beefing up the single-cylinder, inlet-over-exhaust engine to a stalwart 494 ccs in 1906. Then, in 1907, leading link forks were added, giving the model improved handling that was so successful the same design was retained until the development of the Hydra-Glide Harley in 1949. Also, crucially, the crude leather belt drive was replaced by a more maintenance-free chain drive.

This bike pointed the way to the familiar configuration and look that would be reinforced in the following decades. At the same time, the simple frame reveals its origins—the metamorphosis from bicycle with engine

to full-fledged motor-cycle had only begun. Seen here without the benefit of restoration, this 1913 Harley has a raw-boned magnificence.

The name "Silent Gray Fellow" was bestowed by designers William Harley and Arthur Davidson on all the bikes their company produced up to World War I. "Silent" referred to the efficient, sound-squelching mufflers with which the early Harleys were equipped. "Gray" was for the flat gray paint job that distinguished these bikes. "Fellow" was intended to invoke the dependability of the machine. Harleys were built to be sturdy companions on the road, and they were.

EARLY OVERHEAD

1915
Pope

A bicycle manufacturer since the 1870s, Colonel Pope began building motorcycles in 1902. By the teens Popes had developed into heavy dependable mounts known as the "Champion of the Hills." In design and performance the Pope matched any motorcycle in the world.

The Pope's unholy speed was due to its fully overhead-valve (OHV) 61 cubic inch engine. In the early years of the American motorcycle industry OHV engines appeared on just a few designs: the Pope, the Jefferson/P.E.M., the Royal, and the Cyclone—this last one having an overhead-cam!

In spite of its popularity and advanced design, the Pope fell victim to the motorcycle industry's decline after 1913. The last Popes were built in 1918, when the company went back to its bicycle roots. Its 100-year anniversary was celebrated in 1977. But the glory days as builder of an early overhead were

long past. There would be no production of an OHV V-twin in America until Harley-Davidson stunned the riding public in 1936 with its EL model. By then improved highways and better gas brought out the full potential of the OHV. Pope and other early prophets of the overhead engine had foretold the future.

The twenties was the era of the flapper, the martini, jazz, and the great release that followed the First World War. Playing right into the style of these fast moving times, this twin is one of Indian's most popular machines ever. As its styling and brilliant red paint job suggest, the bike was built for speed with panache. The distinctive rhomboid gas tank has been slightly flattened and rounded, and the magnificent cherry-red tubular

RESTORATION THAT GLOWS

1923
Indian Scout

frame cradles a very competitive twin-cylinder power plant.

Period details abound on this classic example. The leaf-sprung front wheel was typical for Indians of the time. Other period details are the frame-mounted control levers, both for gear shifting and throttling, and leather-covered cables. White tires were the standard issue on 1920s motorcycles. The tires were reinforced with white zinc oxide, instead of with carbon black as is done

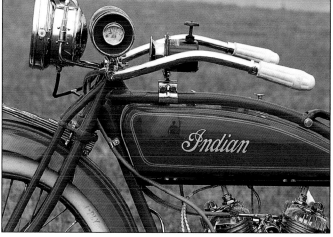

today. As the thirties rolled around the tougher—and more familiar—black tires would take over.

Another standard feature is the big brass head lamp, and its attendant acetylene tank—one of the really attractive features of this exquisite machine. Acetylene lamps became bigger in the twenties as they were forced to compete with electric headlights. Mounted directly behind the headlamp is a classic klaxon horn, whose harsh bray gave Indian a distinctive war whoop on the road.

This bike's restoration differs from a showroom model of 1923 in the high gloss of the nickel-plated engine parts, which would most likely not have been polished to such an extent in that era. In those days nickelplating had a duller look, and the shine one expects today could only be achieved through labor intensive handwork. This work has been done at the restorer's discretion. This machine seems happy to be alive.

ARTILLERY
WITH CANOE
1924
Harley-Davidson JD
and Sidecar

With 74 cubic inches of displacement, this Harley twin offered stiff competition for the Henderson Four, even in the rough business of hauling sidecars.

The elegant "canoe" sidecar on this model is somewhat less sturdy than the military version, but the "artillery" steel wheels are exactly what the Army ordered. Both the steel wheels and the green color continued long after Harleys returned to civilian transport.

The last year for the square tank and loop frame that had characterized Harley from its beginning up through World War I was 1924. A new era was dawning, and as jazz came into its own, the Silent Gray Fellow had begun to look a little stiff. All that would change soon enough.

GROUNDBREAKER
1924
Deluxe Henderson K

Manufactured after 1917 by Ignaz Schwinn's Excelsior Motor Co. of Chicago, Hendersons were without a doubt the standard to match in big, muscular, four-cylinder cycles. This model has an air-cooled, side-valve engine of 65 cubic inch displacement. As redesigned by Arthur Lemon, standard equipment included electric lighting, gear primary drive, and wet sump lubrication —each one an advanced development.

Brother to the Ace Four and the Indian Four, the Henderson K was considered to be the Rolls Royce of motorcycles, and the most highly developed motorcycle ever built.

The machine had a clutch and two-speed transmission with manual starting, in a time when many bikes were still belt-driven single-speeders, started in moped fashion, by vigorous pedaling. The result was a generous package that was well-anointed with modern features.

Although this bike was praised for its groundbreaking design, it is interesting to note that Harley-Davidson, America's only surviving motorcycle company, never once ventured to build a four-cylinder machine. The popularity of power in an American bike has never been disputed. A big country, traversed by seemingly endless stretches of highway, almost demands big four-cylinder bikes.

But somehow Harley sensed what other companies did not—that the big V-twin, rather than an in-line four-cylinder approach—is the American paragon in motorcycle engines. However, this in-line four-cylinder arrangement survived on various makes of motorcycle up until 1941, when Indian made their last four-cylinder machine, and thus sealed the prosperous future of the V-twin forever.

FOUR-CYLINDER WONDER

1926

Ace

The classic look of this powerful four-cylinder, with its set of four downswept pipes and elegant lozenge-shaped gas tank, is the work of a pair of motorcycle siblings—the Henderson brothers. William and Tom Henderson built their first four-cylinder under an eponymous company, which they left to start the Ace organization in 1919.

The bike shown here is the Hendersons' own refinement of their extremely popular earlier bikes. It also served to bring this design to its pinnacle, the 1927 Indian, when that company absorbed Ace a year after this machine was built.

The lustrous beauty of the exposed metal on the Ace comes

from its period nickel plating, enhanced by the restored pinstriping and is on the black-painted metalwork. Technical features that put this Ace ahead of its time are the splash lubrication, the Schebler Deluxe carburetor, and the more than sufficient breaking power provided by the dual rear brakes.

In 1923, Red Wolverton made motorcycle history when he captured the record speed of 123 miles per hour on a specially turned version of the Ace Four. Ace offered the trophy cup from the race, together with prize money, to any challenger who could beat the Ace's achievement. The prize was never claimed.

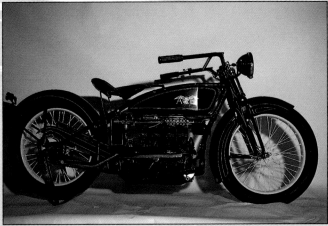

ULTIMATE F-HEAD
1928
Harley-Davidson JDH

This motorcycle shows the final expression of Harley-Davidson's long affair with the F-head engine. Since 1903, improvements had been steady and predictable. In 1911 a V-twin model was adopted. In 1914 kickstart and floorboards were added. In 1915 a three-speed transmission was offered. In 1921 the big 74 cubic inch engine came along—especially favored for sidecar or solo high speed work.

By the twenties, however, Harley-Davidsons were assuming a somewhat antiquated flavor. While Indian and Excelsior had adopted more flowing lines, H-D retained its "square" gas tanks and high frame.

This changed in 1925 with a bold new look. A redesigned frame and streamline tanks imparted a shape familiar even today. Modern Harley-Davidson styling was starting to evolve.

In 1928 riders were offered the option of the JH (61") or JDH (74") engines. These were the famous "two-cam" motors previously available only to competition riders. This hot F-head was H-D's final development of the type. Combined with quick acceleration was a top end of 85-90 mph, although prolonged high speed running invited

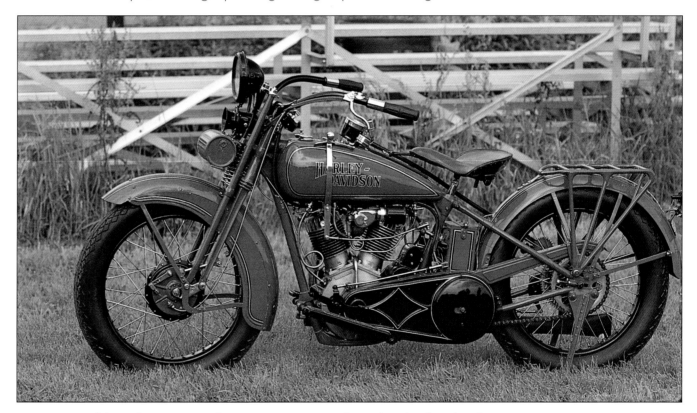

engine trouble. That year riders were given a front brake for the first time—although most shunned using it.

In 1930 the F-head was replaced by a new big twin: the VL. This side-valve engine was similar to what Indian had been building for years. Early troubles with the new Flathead were compounded by the onset of the Great Depression. In 1931, when Ignaz Schwinn dropped out of the motorcycle game, only two American makes were left—Indian and Harley-Davidson—and both of these were driven to the brink of ruin.

HEAVENLY TRANSPORT

1934

Ariel VG500 Deluxe

After languishing in a barn for nearly half a century, this bike took a year to resurrect. The job provided enough work for a team of restorers—each with his own role. There was a high water mark on the outside of the primary cover; rust cloaked on nearly every exposed part; replacement pieces needed for the gear shift knob, tire pump correct throttle, and grips; and there were strange problems with the piston. The task of reviving the Ariel would take surgery, detective work, and rocket science.

One aspect in the restorers' favor was the fact that the subject was a nearly perfect specimen: an absolutely stan-

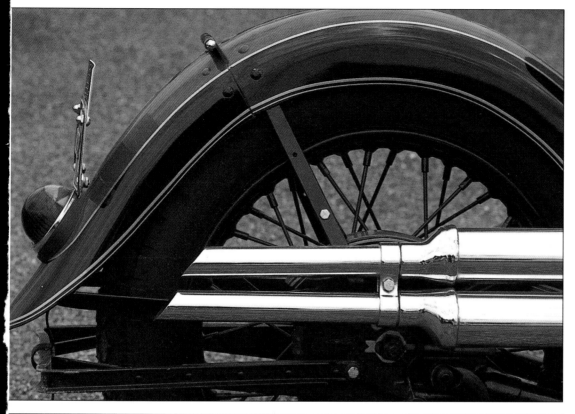

UNLUCKY
INDIAN
1936
Indian Four

dard Ariel Deluxe with all its parts. Because it was mostly all there, little research needed to be done other than the usual gruelling quest for such bits as the "eight day" clock (on the upper left of the instrument panel), which needed to be wound every eight days. Also needed were tank pads and the gearshift knob. Still, this machine is almost completely what it was, when it was rolled out of the barn, from the original piston down to the main bearings and spark plug.

The VG500 Deluxe was a cut below Ariel's top-of-the-line Red Hunter and a cut above its Standard. With its big touring fenders, twin port single-cylinder with twin fishtail exhausts—

something else the restorers had to secure—and 4-speed tank shift, it was both more powerful and more attractive than the Standard.

Those deeply valanced fenders certainly do set it apart, as does the chrome panelling on the gas tank. But the most appealing aspect of this bike is its low, lean, wasplike profile. Like a Victorian dream machine, this Ariel has magic and grace, almost the suggestion of power uncoiling like a striking snake. The all-black components—fenders, spokes, girders—set off the few chromed details to give a sense that is at once utilitarian and, well, deluxe. The machine has fast elegance that shows in the back-swept fenders and 100-mile-per-hour speedometer.

While 1934 was clearly a good year for Ariels, 1994 was even better for this one. Restored perhaps even beyond its former glory, its engine has roared to life once more and its sleek hide has the glow that comes only from lavish care and attention.

This is one machine that repays the attention—tenfold.

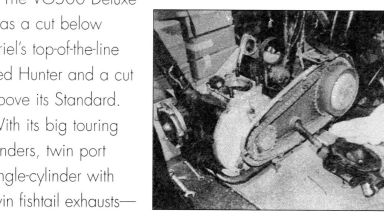

This motorcycle was one of Indian's big mistakes—the "upside-down" Four.

Before WWII four-cylinder motorcycles were favored by some American riders. While V-twins were just as fast, they were prone to heavy vibration. At high speed Fours were glassy smooth. They were the darlings of some police forces.

Having bought the Ace Four in 1927, Indian kept its engine intact until 1936 while giving it their own frame and forks. That year Indian reversed the previous inlet-over-exhaust valve layout for exhaust-over-inlet— hence the term "upside-down" Four. An increase in power

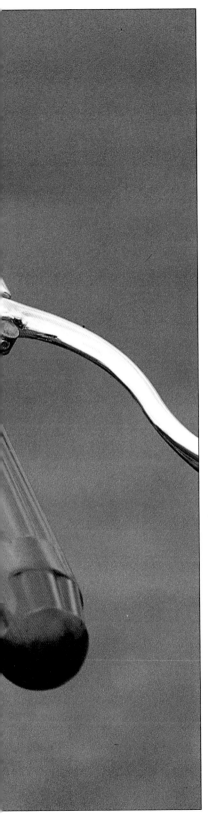

was reported from this 77 cubic inch engine, but at the cost of reliability and an engine picky Four enthusiasts considered grotesque. It

coincided with the reversal of fortunes for the Indian and Harley-Davidson companies. In 1936 H-D introduced its most successful

For reasons known only to Indian management, that company retained the antiquated side-valve engine in their V-twin line. After the Second

twin had evolved into the machine seen on this page—the Hydra-Glide—a second generation OHV V-twin commonly called the Panhead.

was replaced in 1938 with a more conventional engine —the last of the American Fours.

The timing of the "upside-down" Four

model: the EL or "Sixty-One"—also called the Knuckle-head. This overhead-valve V-twin set a new standard in performance and styling.

World War, Indian placed its bets on smaller OHV vertical twins and singles. These failed to catch on. By then the Harley-Davidson big

By the mid-fifties, it was the sole production V-twin in America and in its improved form, is still available today. Indian was dead.

WAR BIKES
1942
U.S. Army Harley-Davidson

The army version of the 1942 Harley had a swagger and an air of danger to it—not undercut at all by the Thompson submachine gun mounted in the scabbard on its fork. Two examples of the military Harleys appear above and below. The lower one was intended for action in North Africa in 1943; it was specially equipped with a sand-resistant shaft drive, but the action was over by the time it was ready. America ordered 88,000 of the upper model for the Second World War. This Harley was a symbol both of the strong character of Mr. Davidson himself and of the climax of his company's long struggle to finally dominate Indian.

In the days before America entered the war, the U.S. Army approached both Indian and Harley-Davidson, the only American motorcycle companies to survive the Great Depression. What the army asked for was a design for a 500 cc military motorcycle. The winner of the plum Army contract would be the company to build the best cycle to the military specs.

Indian began work right away and produced the machine, a civilized model of which appears right. But Mr. Davidson stopped the army in its tracks. No military bike could be of any use at such a ridiculously low power. Davidson said he wouldn't even consider building such a puny bike. The military were blunt—build it, or see your company fail. The bike he did build, with a generous 45 cubic inches of displacement, became the single most beloved motorcycle to come out of the war.

While Indian's military bike was the progenitor of their successful Scout, it was not a success with the troops. Much of the Indian company's contribution to the war effort consisted in making small components such as the Norden bombsight. Later problems of retooling and readjusting to the post-war marketplace would finally doom Indian. They would last just three more short years into the fifties.

MASS MARKET TRANSPORT

1946

Schwinn Whizzer

The Whizzer was a refined throwback. In a year that gave the world some of the most muscular and fully evolved motorcycles it had ever seen, from the Indian Chiefs to the streetwise Gilera Saturno, Schwinn elected to build what was essentially a refinement of a turn-of-the-century idea, bonding a motor to the frame of a bicycle.

There is a pleasing simplicity in the bike shown here. The Marathon frame is sturdy and looks like good, clean fun. The components are well-made and are both sporty and utilitarian. While this bike would never produce a tremendous amount of speed, speed was not its raison d'etre. When the Whizzer rolled off the line, consumerism was just taking wing and the age of disposable income was dawning. This was a machine that promised a kind of utility—what better vehicle for a quick hop to the corner store? But, in fact, it represented an entree into the thrilling world of motorcycling at minor expense. The example here cost less than $100 when new, though it now fetches nearer to $4,000.

There is something in the exact shade of blue of the Whizzer tank, and the very forties' typestyle of its cursive logo, that evokes the time for which this bike was built. A World War had just been fought and won. The boys had just come home, and the economy (if not yet the general public) was beginning to rock 'n' roll. With its white balloon tires and harmless looking engine, Schwinn's machine provided an easy way to get up on two wheels and swing.

ITALIAN HEARTBREAKER
1947
Gilera Saturno

The Saturno has rightly been called the most elegant single-cylinder machine in motorcycle history. Most of all, it was the low slung, massive engine casing—seemingly whittled from a single billet of aluminum—slung on a single-loop frame that grabbed the hearts of single-cylinder lovers. The assertiveness of the raked front forks adds to this Saturno's speedy lines, as do the drooping racing handlebars. This is a bike that seems to be moving even when it's not.

With 500 ccs, this sleek racer won fans for both its power on the race track and its good looks on the road. The extreme purity of Saturno's styling, according to some experts, has put it into a class with such Italian motoring legends as the Bugatti Type 35 Grand Prix car. Certainly, in a country that puts style above all else, this machine is an honored achievement.

One look at the distinctive tower, encasing a column of gears beside the cylinder —the Saturno's trademark—and it's easy to see how this high revving, overhead cam engine could tear up the track. Carlo Bandirola rode one of these machines to victory at San Remo in 1947 —a feat that was to be repeated by Gilera riders for the following four years. Ever after these successes, these legendary racers would be known as San Remos.

Features that distinguish this bike include its parallel rear suspension, center-suspended blade-type girder forks, and a single-unit cast gear box. The Saturno also possessed an alloy cylinder and head construction that was rare for its era.

Gilera lasted as a company for sixty years, from its founding in 1909 by twenty-two year old Giuseppe Gilera until it was sold to Piaggio, the maker of the Vespa scooter, in 1969. Part of a line

started in 1939 that included the Mars and the Nettuno, the Saturno was a mainstay of the company's output for twenty years, winning its last championship on the track in 1957, just two years before Gilera halted its production.

Fortunately, the Saturno has reappeared. In 1989, Piaggio renewed the line with the Nuovo Saturno—a completely modern single-cylinder bike along the same lightweight, sporting lines as its predecessor.

CHIEF DELUXE
1947
Indian Chief

From the Indian Chief mascot light on its front fender to the decal on its rear skirts, this bike is original down to its nuts and bolts—a rare find. Like the Harley model of 1947, the Indian Chief's engine displaced 74 cubic inches—enough power to move its 550 pounds around with grace and ease. A luxurious ride was ensured by plunger rear suspension—the competition had no rear suspension at all at this time—and low-pressure balloon tires. Later Chiefs (there would be Indian Chiefs up until 1953) grew still more sumptuous.

The comfort and visual extravaganza offered by Indian was not as central to

Harley's philosophy —speed and power were. While the bikes had roughly the same size engines, what they did with all those cc's was ultimately what would lead to Harley's rise and Indian's fall. Any Indian bike lover will tell you it is precisely those differences from Harley that make these machines attractive: classic American creations, each one an original.

This model was the quintessential Indian Chief, the bike that Indian threw into the all-out war with Harley-Davidson for control of the American motorcycle market. This war began back in the midst of motorcycle history, but intensified when Indian and

Harley became the only American motorcycle companies to emerge alive from the dark days of the Great Depression. Harley's post-war sales strategy emphasized big machines and was extremely successful, while Indian divided its time and money between its accepted classic models and some new designs which eventually failed.

This machine exemplifies the highest pitch of Indian's unique style, in the company's long, post-heyday period. There is something at once archaic and deeply impressive about the skirted and valanced fenders—the first design elements to which the eye is drawn. Then there are the straight girder front forks and elegant, windswept chrome strips waving back over both fenders. The single big headlight is also attention grabbing, and of course the teardrop gas tank. But you could get that with Harley. For many, it was precisely the differences that Indian offered that made it a dream machine.

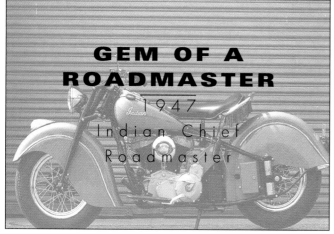

GEM OF A
ROADMASTER

1947
Indian Chief
Roadmaster

Beautifully restored from its former condition, this bike is a near-perfect example of the '47 Roadmaster. It is a long road from the rusted, disassembled parts with which so many of these restorations begin to the gleaming product seen here. The payoff? This bike would have sold for $700 to $800 in 1947; it is now worth somewhere around $15,000.

There is hardly a motorcycle as seductively stylish as the 1947 Indian Chief. The exquisite Cajun-green finish of this particular bike was actually offered by the factory. Adding to the machine's authenticity are the wide tires that gave the Roadmaster its celebrated easy ride. These were made from the original Armstrong molds, now used by major tire companies specifically to serve the burgeoning Indian restoration market.

The art of restoration can be both tricky and time-consuming. While there are books on the subject, few are reliable. One might then ask what authorities exist to ensure that a particular model of bike is accurately restored —what records or publications detail the technical and stylistic specifics intensively enough to serve as a guide? For the most part, the intrepid restorer must dig for first-hand knowledge by talking to those who know: people at meets, former mechanics and factory workers— sometimes even the model's designers, if they are still alive.

To bring this motorcycle back from its degraded state to its present pristine condition, genuine parts were located or painstakingly copied, multiple layers of paint stripped, and a year's worth of intensive effort was put into bringing these nuts and bolts into the working, showroom-floor quality expected in a top-class restoration.

TRICKED OUT FOR CRUISING

1947

Indian Chief

This 1947 Indian Chief represents a critical turning point in the history of its legendary manufacturer. The year 1948 was the last for the Indian Chief until a disastrous year without these beauties on the market persuaded Indian to go back on line with them in 1950. This gap in production was just one of a number of crucial missteps made by the Indian company that would eventually lead to its ruin in 1953.

The elaborately tricked-out saddle seen on this model was typical of the many options offered on Indian Chiefs of this time. For a few extra dollars—$10.00 here, $7.00 there, the buyer could add the little details that make a bike unique. Leather saddlebags, a frequent addition, were also used on Harleys of the period. In fact, without the deep curtaining of the Indian fenders, it would be difficult for the untutored eye to find the essential difference between the competing Harley and the Indian Chief.

The likenesses between Harleys and Indians only sharpened the competition between the two companies. Brand loyalty was so sought by these companies that the bikes were designed to encourage it. Switching bikes could even have proved dangerous up until the late thirties, as each company put its throttle and gear shift on a different side, and gave a different function to the forward or rearward movement of the clutch pedal. Few indeed were the bikers who could move from one machine to the other without winding up in a hospital.

In time, this practice was forced to a halt by the simple requirement of making sales to police forces and the army, which needed a standardized control layout. Today, by international consent, almost all bikes are made with the throttle on the right handlebar, gearchange at the left foot, and clutch on the left handlebar.

Since Indian's demise in 1953, various attempts have been made to revive the venerable Indian

marque. In fact, there is a movement afoot to do so today. Thus far, these forays have all been as ill-fated as the original, although even a Harley aficionado will tell you Indian had a long proud run, one that lives on in legendary bikes like this one.

SIX HUNDRED POUNDS OF LUXURY

1951

Indian Chief Roadmaster

Here we see the Indian Chief Roadmaster near the apex of its development. Weighing in at over 600 pounds, the 1951 Roadmaster was the heaviest bike Indian ever produced. Perhaps it had something to do with the fashion in cars Detroit was turning out in the postwar years, which tended to be heavy on the sheet metal. But there is much more to this bike—the last of the true Indians—than sheer bulk. This bike is so well built and so thoughtfully designed that it might almost be called over-engineered.

The Roadmaster's luxurious ride is accented by innovations such as the telescopic front forks,

which superseded the blade girders on the previous chief in 1950. The larger 80 cubic inch engine was an upgrade that was introduced that same year. The lit-from-within Indian mascot head on the front fender was standard from 1947 until the final Chief rolled off the assembly line in 1953.

On this shining example, the restorer paired a fine factory sea foam blue with a gleaming white finish. Although it's not 100 percent

technically accurate, the restorer's choice gives this motorcycle a look that says 1951 Roadmaster.

The long chummy seat seen on this model is the standard version offered by reproduction companies and differs little from the original. And the front wheel speedometer, which would be phased out at year's end, was nonetheless ideal for informing a bold rider of just how hard he was riding this powerful machine.

1952 Harley-Davidson Hydra-Glide

LAST OF THE CHIEFS
1952
Indian Chief
Roadmaster

The long bench seat of this massive bike represents one of the last significant developments to come along for the Indian Chief before it passed into history—and out of production—a year later. Another last-minute innovation was the low-slung, fishtail exhaust.

There is a reason for the Roadmaster's prominence during the fifties and a contemporary attention to it. This bike is an example of the allure. The eye can't seem to get enough of that big, 80 cubic-inch V-twin, enough of the coiled and curving crash bars, enough of the swept fenders. Each surviving Indian offers homage to a departed era: America's golden age of motorcycle cruising.

There's no question that Harleys have an inordinate amount of style. And Harleys survived, where as Indian didn't, so overall, Harleys have to be given more credit. But the Indian carved out its niche in motorcycling legend, and it did it with a look that has never been matched.

This is a style that just may have been too lush, too quintessential for its time, to be able to endure beyond its time.

The Roadmaster went out like a comet. If it died young, it left a good-looking corpse.

JAMPOT
SINGLE
1954
AJS 18CS

This AJS has been restored to replicate precisely the type of AJS that could have been found roaring across a patch of desert in southern California in the fifties. These AJS 500 cc bikes were popular because they were tough as well as fast, and when mounted with dirt bike tires, there was almost no maneuver that they couldn't accomplish once they had a gutsy rider on board.

For many bikers, particularly American and English, the words "jampot single" conjure a vision that conforms exactly to the bike shown here. "Jampot" refers to the sturdy, squat rear shocks. Single, is, of course, in reference to the massive, lone cylinder. What the two words together mean: A competition dirt-racing scrambler that took America's west coast by storm in the 1950s and 1960s. These

bikes tore up back roads and dirt hills all over England and California well before Yamaha or Suzuki ever fielded a moto-cross bike, much less captured the market. In fact, when Britain's a few features the British versions and full-fledged dirt bikes don't. For example, the gearing is set for the road, not the out-back, so the rider can take it on cross-country jaunts that

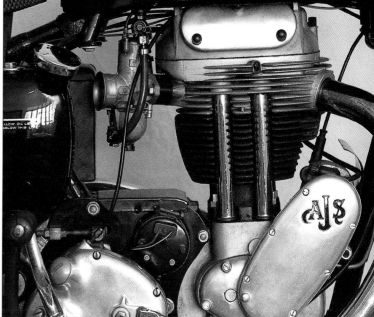

AMC firm built this machine they were the largest motorcycle company in the world.

This is definitely a bike for riding, and despite its age, it has plenty of miles left in it. To that end it has stretch as far as New York to Georgia. This feature illustrates yet another form of collecting, in which the owner tailors his restoration to give him a bike he can take out on the road.

HEART OF
A ROCKET
1955

Triumph Tiger
110

The streamlined headlight nacelle on this sea shell blue Tiger represents a classic Triumph feature that distinguished all Triumph bikes of this period. One look over the tank-top luggage rack and the gauges embedded in black metal testifies to the

enduring popularity—and surpassing fame—of the Triumph marque.
This view was revolutionary in 1955 and remains elegant today.

   The Tiger 110 spawned a tradition of speed, and fast-living was
a buzzword of the fifties. This bike has a 650 cc powerplant, the
same engine which, with a few modifications and cowled in a
rocket-shaped body, blew Johnny Allen to an unofficial but impressive

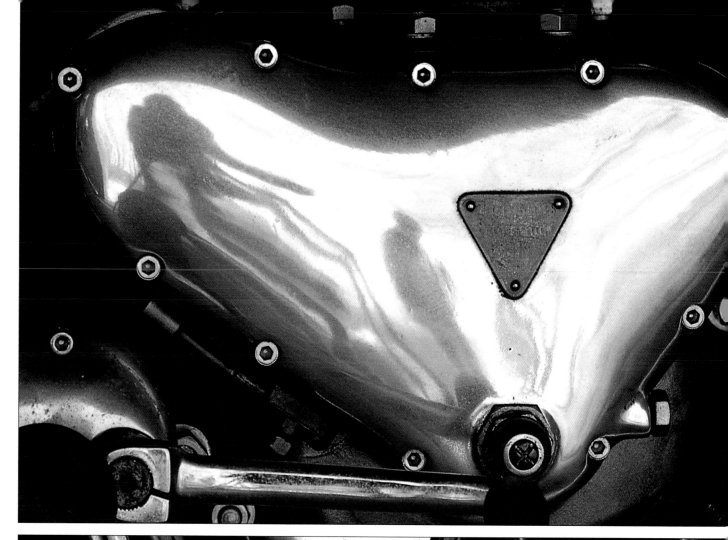

motorcycle speed record in 1956—214.4 miles per hour. With the addition of a second carburetor, the Tiger would become the Bonneville, named for the very salt flats on which the record was set.

Comparing this bike with its fellow Triumphs, it's easy to see how the company held the field against all comers for so many years—consistent, dynamic styling that holds up over decades and never looks dated.

MUSEUM
QUALITY
1962
Triumph
TR6 SS Trophy

Some may think the tank badge design on this Triumph goes a bit over the top, but if it looks proud, this TR6 has a right to be. It's a museum or "concours" quality restoration. It's a bike, in other words, at the peak of restored condition, authentic to the nuts and bolts. "Concours" quality means that this motorcycle can compete in the rigorously judged European restoration events that bear that name. This example is also a "matching

numbers" job: the serial numbers on frame and engine are the same, indicating the basic machine is a factory original.

The TR6 Trophy is essentially the most well-known Bonneville, but with one carburetor instead of two. Some traditionalists frowned on the Bonnie's twin carbs, which could be fussy if maladjusted. This is the last of the non-unit-construction 650s, whose engines and gearboxes are the last of the pre-units, joined by the time-honored engine plates. Ever afterward, Triumph would incorporate the close-coupled look of unit construction.

THAT NORTON
LOOK
1965

Norton 650SS
Dominator

Built from 1962 until 1970, the Dominator was a classic British bike of the sixties. With its characteristic chrome fenders, an enclosed chain case, and upright parallel twin cylinders, it was a common sight around London in the very turbulent days of Beatlemania.

Details that always distinguish a Norton, aside from the antique look of the proud tank badge, is the feather bed frame as well as the slightly humped, flat-on-bottom gas tank, and the Norton road-holder patented forks.

It was the consistent successs of the Triumph Speed Twin, produced in 1937, that led to the arrival of the Dominator. Norton decided to come out with their own rival twin, a 500 cc parallel they built in 1948. Every twin the company was to build for the next thirty years would be based on this original design, giving Nortons a look-alike quality that has served to distinguish them from other British bikes.

BRITISH TRADITION

1965

Royal Enfield Interceptor

From the crisp, imperial tank badge to the striking bright blue paint job, this carefully restored bike exemplifies the straightforward styling of British motorbikes. In the case of the Interceptor, the motor itself is an integral part of the frame. With its heavily finned head and paired vertical cylinders, the 737cc Interceptor welded power to beauty.

Stressed-member engines were standard issue at British companies in the early thirties and became popular with companies in Europe and in America from then on. Royal Enfield in particular made its grand, solid engine construction its trademark, produc-

ing castings that seemed hewn from granite and were mounted low in the frame. Such sturdy construction was also typical of British bikes of the period.

Just two years after this splendid bike was made, Royal Enfield's English factory shut down, a victim of the fierce

competition provided by Japanese bikes. Many motorcyclists lamented the demise of such great British bike builders as Royal Enfield, and pointed to the inferior Japanese construction of that time—the very nuts and bolts of the frames were likely to snap off under hard use. Even though the early technical problems of the Japanese bikes have been overcome, negative terms are still used by some die-hards to disparage the Japanese machines.

Royal Enfields were still produced in India in the late eighties. A model called the Bullet is used by the Indian police and military—though the tank badge has been conveniently abbreviated to "Enfield."

STREET RACER

1966

Triumph TT

Special

The sylvan surroundings of this bike belie its real use: street racing. This dangerous, even deadly, pasttime flourished in New York in the early seventies, as various groups from the city's five boroughs competed for big money. This bike emerged during a time when the boundary between fine and popular arts were blurred as American society and culture strove to redefine itself through informality and exaggeration.

"Hot rodding" bred its own requirements in a bike. This Triumph has been modified to a fair-thee-well. From the Dunstall glass tank and exhausts to the Ceriani front forks and owner-modified oil tank, this machine sports components normally only seen on legitimate racing bikes. The close ratio gear box is one of the few factory parts, and it's a rarity.

Black is a thoroughly appropriate color for this speed machine. It has the look of a bandit. Just compare it to other '66 Triumphs to get an idea of just how cranked up it is. And yet, despite all this custom work, its lean line and whipcrack looks say Triumph in every line.

The TT Special was so-named because of the suitability of the Triumph for a type of U.S. dirt-track racing that is called TT.

This Triumph TT is a symbol of Triumph's past involvement in racing, as well as of a particularly daring era of speed when these bikes raced on the mean streets of New York City.

BUILT FOR SPEED

1967

Triumph Bonneville

The Bonneville name owes its origin to the salt flats in Utah, in the United States, where a 650 cc Triumph broke the World Land Speed record. Although the record was disputed, slapping this name on their bikes gave Triumph the last laugh.

With the launching of the new Triumph in 1990, the laughter continued. Like its brother Triumphs, this machine exemplifies British bike-making at its best. Although not an especially remarkable model, this Bonneville is an excellent cross

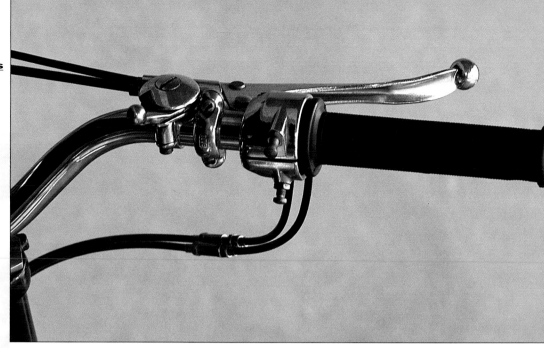

section of the company's output. It would take everything the Japanese could do in the fiercely competitive market of the seventies to topple and almost destroy the tradition that Triumph had put together. But the tradition was upheld and allowed to live on when, in the midst of that embattled decade, Triumph employees occupied the factory and refused to let it close. Their worker's cooperative eventually crumbled in 1983, but the spirit hung on, to be revived in 1990 when production resumed at a factory in Leicestershire, England, using designs inspired by the Japanese.

TRIUMPH
MADE UNDER
PATENT NOS
713,932 721,073
684,685 647,670
475,860
469,635

BLACK BEAUTY
1968
BMW R69/2 with
R75/6 Motor

When this bike was built the fabric of American society seemed to be coming apart at the seams—what with the riots at the Democratic Convention in Chicago, Vietnam protests, and raucous rock concerts across the country as the Hippie culture moved like a juggernaut towards Woodstock. In the midst of this wild scene, the R69 was an island of buttoned-down tradition.

Although the engine on this bike was built in 1975, the basic design remains unchanged from the original powerplant built over half a century earlier—the famous horizontal flat twin. Also called the "Boxer," because of the brisk, horizontal jabbing action of its pistons, this engine became the hallmark of a BMW—the massive cylinder heads bulging out on each side in the head-on view becoming a classic silhouette.

The timeless look —and staggering

beauty of this BMW and sidecar has its origins in the Bavarian Motor Works commitment to creating beauty through efficiency, or so the owner might explain. Any doubts on this score can be set to rest by one glance at the simple instrument layout laid into the crisply rectilinear gas tank. Everything that the rider needs is there, neatly in its place. This R69 is a graphic example of the kind of clean industrial design that Germany became famous for in the thirties.

The military-looking sidecar shown here is actually Russian, though BMW did issue a sidecar as standard equipment up until the late sixties. The Ural, as it is known, does have a very German pedigree, however. Its basic design was copied by the Russians from captured German sidecars during the Second World War. The only characteristically Russian feature is the fender light.

Ducati was yet another company that entered the motorcycle market early on with modified bicycles, only to undergo a revolution in 1954 when designer Fabio Taglioni joined the firm. Taglioni introduced a number of technological marvels to Ducati bikes, including a superb single cylinder, overhead camshaft engine that was first used on the company's racing bikes and later on its road versions.

Here is a cobbling together of several eras in Ducati design, with the 1968 chassis featuring the later desmodromic valve, single cylinder of a 1974 450 cc bike, together with the later telescopic forks.

THE NAME THAT SAYS SPEED
1968/1974 Ducati

Although the machine shown here is now somewhat outdated,
this powerful single was a legend on the racing circuit for more than
a decade, and established a name for Ducati that still sells bikes —
though they are now a good deal more powerful than this one.

MARKET
BOOSTER

1975
Norton 850 Commando
Roadster

Norton's problem in 1969 was to somehow tame the shaking of its high-vibration, parallel-twin engine, to match the smoothness of Japanese machines. Their answer was Isolastic mounting, which allowed the engine to move without either transmitting its shaking to the rider or destroying Norton's fine handling qualities. To stay in the high-performance game, the engine was enlarged —first to 750, then to 850 cc—and electric starting was added.

Clever though they were, these extemporizations could not compensate for the company's lack of modern designs or production facilities. Today's Norton, a victim of financial shenanigans, barely clings to life despite offering an innovative and potent Wankel rotary-powered machine.

THE BEST
BOXER EVER

1981-1984

BMW Standard R100

Swift, adept, and powerful, this machine has been hailed by many BMW aficionados as the best flat twin this Bavarian company ever built. Looking at the lean lines of this creature, captured in its natural environment, this assessment would be hard to argue with. After all, the bike has everything that makes BMWs great. With 100 ccs it serves as a stalwart tourer, in the proud tradition of its predecessors. And with the trademark twin cylinders thrusting out on either side, it retains the famous profile despite many design innovations.

To accommodate the owner's individual style, this motorcycle has many customized parts from the 1981-1984 BMW Standard R100 models. In this case the owner added: a windshield, fork gators, an after-market exhaust system,

and low European-style handlebars. Many owners modify their bikes to suit their riding needs, whatever their needs might be!

BEAUTY AND THE BEAST
1983
Laverda RGS 1000 Executive

From almost every angle, this bike reflects the high-tech vision of its designers, and the innate artistic genius of Italian bodywork. The striking cutaway of the fairing, and the sculptural fantasy of this bike's cowlings and panniers leave streamlining behind and head into the territory of biomorphism.

Much more than a visual feast, the elegant fabric of this Laverda conceals a monster of power. Three cylinders house nearly 1000 cubic centimeters of displacement, capable of 90 brake horse power. The tuned version of this massive triple, the Jota, was the fastest production bike available in the late seventies.

While the Executive was hailed for its sophisticated design, this bike would also become notorious as one of the most unstable and difficult-to-ride street bikes ever produced. Anything close to fast speed produced nasty shaking from the handle bar ends and pegs. Moreover, the tall engine had a tendency to knot up in curves and lay the bike over excessively.

Perhaps the celebrated power—and noise, bulk, and excessive vibration—of Laverdas can be attributed to the company's original product, agricultural machinery. Or perhaps not. In any case, though the company still has a reputation for big,

solidly made bikes of great speed and racing performance, the Jota faded from the scene in the green eighties, and the streets became a quieter place. Although the Executive was only manufactured for a couple of years, it is a fine example of the brutally powerful machines for which Laverda became famous.

DIRT TRACK
MONSTER
1986
Harley-Davidson
XR 750

This custom racing bike roared into history almost as soon as it was built. Constructed by Mert Lawmill, it was originally raced by world champions Wayne Rainey, Chris Carr, Steve Morehead, Ricky Graham, and Dan Ingram. It began winning races in 1986 and by 1987 it had set the record for the fastest lap ever recorded on a dirt track—104.312 miles per hour. This record has only recently been broken.

This bike is a perfect example of a dirt track race bike. Most dirt track races, the most popular motorcycle sport in America, are held on half-mile (800 m) and one-mile (1.6 km)

tracks. Designed to tear around a continuous left turn at breakneck speeds, there is a barely visible gap between the right fork and hub while the tire nearly touches the fork on the inside. Tolerances on machines such as this one are set so acutely that a single fall can sideline the bike for months. While it bears little resemblance to road Harleys, the bike exemplifies the spirit of that company in its awesome speed and power— the two elements that kept Harley-Davidson in business when the Japanese came knocking in the sixties with machines so powerful that the British were all but driven from the market.

The aluminum cylindered XR 750 engine that powers this bike was the product of rule changes in 1968 allowing a more powerful dirt track bike. After extensive redesigns over the years, it has earned a great name among dirt trackers.

Aspects to notice about this model are the Italian Ceriani front forks, the lack of any front hub braking—typical for oval track racers— and the screws on the tire rims, which prevent any movement of the tire through excess torque when accelerating or braking.

The massive can muffler is standard issue on racing bikes, allowing the engine to develop greater

than normal compression at the cost of excessive noise. Proper exhaust tuning is essential to racing engine performance.

TRANSVERSE TWIN
1993
Moto Guzzi 1200
California

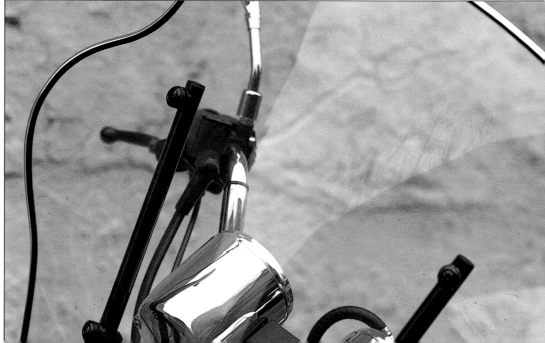

Here is a bike that is emblematic of the year it was first offered: 1993. With a naked, open-air design that is reminiscent of the glory days of motorcycle building, here is a machine that goes back to basics from the overblown 1980s. This 1993 model also says a lot about the company that built it.

The tank is globular, yet sleek, and the styling harkens back to a time when the engine was not something to hide but the very essence of a bike's look.

The V-twin is Moto Guzzi's recognition point, the tag that

says "Italian." The world-class designers of this machine would no sooner cover it with plastic than snip their famous eagle from the tank. It's all about history. The eagle is there because one of the company's founders was a flying ace in World War I. When he didn't make it back from the front, his partners honored him by taking the symbol of the Italian Air Force and appending it to their product. There's been a fighter plane hidden in every Moto Guzzi since then.

From a technical standpoint the engine in this bike is excellent, if not earth-shaking. What really takes it over the top is its styling. Note the beautifully formed clear fairing, edged in waving lines of chrome, and the subtle repeated curves of tank and frame tubing. This is a motorcyle that was sculpted before it was built. Unlike the modern Harleys, which are virtual remakes of the 1949 models, this is a new foray into the old tradition. And in this case, the old tradition has been improved.

WORLD CHAMPION

1993

Ducati 851

Superbike

Red is the Italian racing color—as opposed to the more subdued British racing green—and it does justice to this savage-looking machine. There is a grace in the fine styling and the slightly exposed trellis frame that belies the fearsome 90-degree V-twin with water cooling, eight valves, and fuel injection just beneath the surface. These elements were brought together for the first time ever in a Ducati road machine in 1989, when the first 851 was built.

This bike is known as a world champion, and rightly so. Racing versions of it have won top honors on race tracks all over the world. But what these photos reveal is that the Italian looks are still unmatched, even as the motorcycle metamorphoses into something totally different from the sort of thing the 1993 Moto Guzzi represents—the proud tradition of letting the engine hang out. With the Superbike, biomorphism reigns. As home electronics become more asymmetrical and organic, motorcycles echo the trend. More than streamlining, this fashion in motorcycle design conjures up an animal that just happens to be made of metal, glass and plastic—an animal that eats the road and has gasoline for blood. There is a reason for this evolution, and it has to do with more than style. Successful marketing

of just about any product depends on showing the public something new and exciting.

Look carefully at the seating arrangement on the 851 and you'll see another Ducati trademark—uncomfortable seating. Rider comfort was not a priority when this machine was designed. But then, when going 160 miles per hour, the rider's mind is not on what is "behind" him.

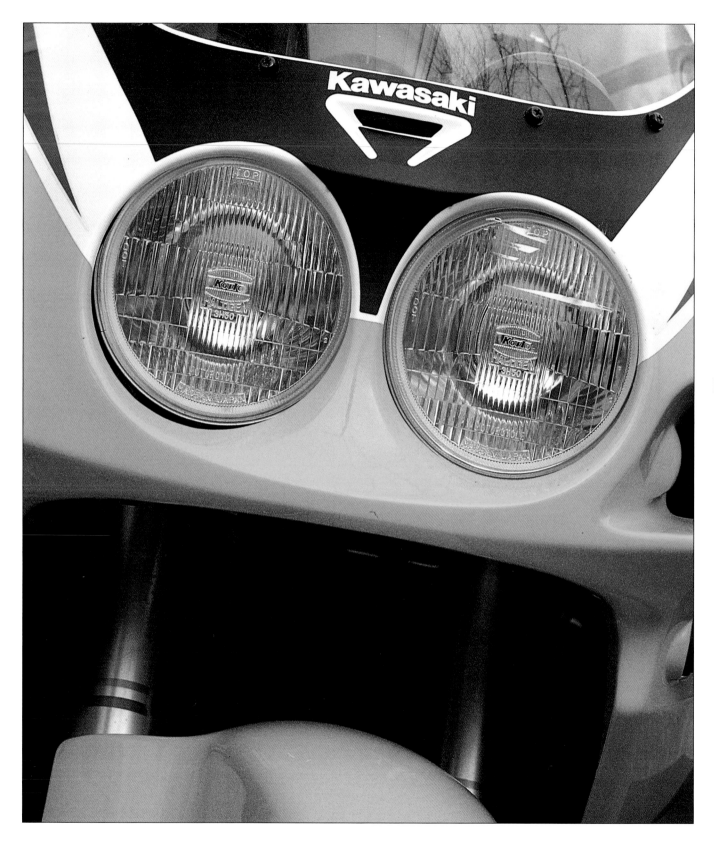

**BEASTIE
BIKE**

1994

Kawasaki
Ninja

The 180 miles per hour shown on this bike's speedometer is not a joke. The bike can move that fast. And not with the Harley's swaggering roar, either.

When wound out, this motorcycle sounds like a very loud vacuum cleaner. It never seems to strain. But for all of its plastic and poster paint colors, the Ninja is no toy. A serious rider is required to keep his mind on his business—and the wheels on the road.

An owner who recently chatted about this bike said he could probably handle the top speed, but that he just didn't want to. This is probably smart. Speed is a very fickle flirt.

Ever since it was first introduced in the 1980s, the Ninja has been a symbol of flat-out speed, and in many ways it is the quintessential contemporary Japanese machine. Something in its overall design—the low-slung body, the molded air-scoops, and nimble wheelbase—suggests the wild, dreamlike fluorescent quality of recent Japanese animated movies.

Glossary

Bonneville Flats An area of the Great Salt Desert in Utah, which, because of its flat terrain, is used for testing speed in vehicles.

Bore The diameter of the engine's cylinder(s). It, together with the stroke determines the engine's displacement.

Boxer Nickname for BMW's horizontal flat twin-cylinder engine.

Cam A largely circular rotating form with a protruding portion that imparts intermittent motion to control the opening and closing of engine valves.

Camshaft The shaft in the engine having cams to operate the valve mechanisms.

Carburetor Instrument for mixing fuel and air into a combustible vapex.

CCs Cubic centimeters. A measure of an engine's displacement, which is the volume swept out by the motion of the pistons.

Chain Drive A drive using chains and sprockets.

Clutch The mechanism connecting the engine crankshaft with the transmission.

Compression Reducing gas volume by squeezing it into a smaller space, consequently increasing the pressure.

Cowling Any type of streamlined enclosure. See fairing.

Cradle Motorcycle frame that places the engine between two frame tubes. See also open cradle and stressed member.

Crankshaft The critical part of the engine that changes the linear movement of the piston into rotational movement.

Cyclometer A device that records a wheel's revolutions; used to record the distance traveled by the vehicle.

Cylinder An open tube in which a piston moves up and down.

Desmodromic Valve A type of valve mechanism that closes the valves with a rocker arm.

Dirt Bike A motorcycle designed for off-road use.

Fairing A front enclosure to improve the bike's aerodynamics or the rider's comfort.

F-head Engine design with one overhead-valve and one side-valve.

Front Fork Section of the motorcycle attatched from the steering head of the frame to the front wheel.

Fuel Injection A fuel-delivery system that sprays fuel under pressure into the intake air valve before it enters the cylinder.

Girder Forks A common form of front suspension on early machines. The front wheel is held in a set of forks that are attached to the steering head by parallel links.

Horsepower A measure of mechanical power, or the rate at which work is done.

Isolastic Engine Mountings Norton's patented form of rubber engine mountings.

Jampot An early type of telescopic rear hydraulic shock absorber, used on AJS-Matchless machines.

Leading-Link Front suspension system in which short links pivot at the bottom of a solid fork. The axle mounts on the front of the link, creating movement of which is controlled by a spring.

Leaf-sprung Front Suspension Any front suspension employing flat leaf springs.

Lubricating System The system supplying engine parts with lubricating oil to prevent contact between metal surfaces.

Marque Product make or brand.

Muffler A device that exhaust gases pass through to deaden their sound.

Nacelle A streamlined enclosure for engine, headlight, etc.

Open Cradle A frame that has no lower frame tubes: the engine is bolted into place becoming part of the frame as a stressed member (the frame is incomplete without the engine).

Overhead-cam Engine design with camshaft and valves placed above the cylinder.

Overhead-valve Engine design with valves placed above the cylinder.

Panniers Packs hung over the motorcycle's rear wheel. Also called saddlebags.

Plunger Rear suspension system where the axle is mounted between two vertical springs.

Port Passage or opening leading to the interior of the cylinder.

Pre-unit Engine and gearbox constructed in separate units, common on older machines.

Shaft Drive A drive using gears and shafts.

Shock Absorber A frictional or hydraulic device provided to damp wheel movement.

Sidecar A passenger car attached to the side of a motorcycle.

Side-valve Engine design with valves placed alongside and parallel to the cylinder. Also called flathead.

Stressed Member Component (usually the engine) that forms part of the whole structure (usually the frame).

Stroke Measurement of the piston's travel, usually expressed in millimeters.

Suspension The system of springs and other parts that supports the motorcycle.

Telescopic forks A type of front wheel suspension in which the up and down motion is provided in telescoping struts.

Throttle The valve that controls the volume of air admitted to the engine's cylinders. The throttle is similar to the automobile's accelerator pedal.

TT Tourist Trophy races at the Isle of Man; in the U.S., a type of dirt track racing.

Tralling-link Similar to leading-link forks, except the link pivots at the front, with the axle mounted at the rear.

Twin Any engine having two cylinders.

Twinport A cylinder-head design that has two ports branching away from a single valve.

Two-stroke Engine An engine in which all events take place in two piston strokes.

Unit Construction Construction of the engine and gearbox within the same castings.

V-Twin A twin-cylinder engine whose cylinders are disposed at an angle to each other (ie. 45, 90, etc.)

Wankel Engine A type of internal combustion rotary engine with two major moving parts.

Services

Restoration and Engine Builders

BIG 4 MOTORCYCLE
ENGINEERING
Redmoor Lane
Newtown
Newmills
Derbyshire SK12 3JL
Tel: 0663 741103

THE BRITISH BIKE SHED
Unit 4
Fairs Road
Leatherhead
Surrey KT22 7PD
Tel: 0372 360858

CAST IRON MOTORS
MOTORCYCLE ENGINEERING
Windmill Farm
Kirby Lodge
Kirby Bellars
Melton Mowbray
Leicestershire LE14 2TH
Tel: 0664 840890

DRAGONFLY MOTORCYCLES
Dept C, Broad Street
Bungay
Suffolk NR35 1EE
Tel: 0986 894798

D.S.M ENGINEERING
Petersfield
Hampshire GU32 IPL
Tel: 0730 823245

EMPIRE MOTORCYCLES
32 Canning Street
Hull
East Yorkshire
Tel: 0482 217104

THE LAVERDA SPECIALISTS
MIURA ENGINEERING LTD
PO Box 620
Chalfont-St.-Giles
Buckinghamshire HP8 4XJ
Tel: 0494 872233

BOB PORECHA
BMW SPECIALIST
303 Sydenham Road
Sydenham
London SE26 5EW
Tel: 081 659 8860

R.E.D.
DEREK ROWLES
Biggleswade MK44 3NS
Tel: 0767 640252

ROBIN JAMES
Clinton Road
Leominster
Herefordshire HR6 ORJ
Tel: 0568 612800

S.E.P.
39 Sideley Road
Kegworth
Derbyshire DE7 2FJ
Tel: 0509 673295

Dealers, Parts and Spares

ALLBIKE SPARES
102-106 Trafalgar Road
Greenwich
London SE10 9UW
Tel: 081 853 5470

ATLANTIC MOTORCYCLES
20 Station Road
Twyford
Berkshire RG10 9NT
Tel: 0734 342266

BERNARD THOMAS
ANTIQUE AMERICAN
MOTORCYCLES
The Barn, Moorside
Old Lindley/Halifax
West Yorkshire HX4 9DF
Tel: 0422 376933

BLAYS OF TWICKENHAM LTD
32-38 The Green
Twickenham
Middlesex TW2 5AB
Tel: 081 894 2103

CARL ROSNER
Station Approach
Sanderstead Road
South Croydon
Tel: 081 657 0121

ECCLES RACING
Unit 7
Cave Industrial Estate
Fen Road
Cambridge CB4 1UN
Tel: 0223 425542

F.H. WARR & SONS LTD
HARLEY-DAVIDSON AGENT
104/106 Waterford Road
Fulham
London SW6
Tel: 071 736 2934

GREENLOOMS CLASSICS
Greenlooms Farm
Hargrave
Chester CH3 7RX
Tel: 0831 202101

ITALSPORT
DUCATI SPECIALISTS
Unit 1, Yarwood Street
Bury
Gtr Manchester BL9 1AU
Tel: 061 797 6124

JEFFREY'S MOTORCYCLES
Hill Cottage Farm
Hogshaw
Quainton, (Nr) Aylesbury
Buckingham MK18 3LA
Tel: 0296 670666

LIGHTNING SPARES
157 Cross Street
Sale
Cheshire M33 7SW
Tel: 061 969 3850

BEN LLOYD MOTORCYCLES
HAWKSHAW MOTORCYCLES LTD
37 Bridge Road
Blundellsands
Liverpool L23 6SA
Tel: 051 924 2369

NORTHANTS CLASSIC BIKE
CENTRE
25 Victoria Street
Irthlingborough NN9 5RG
Northamptonshire
Tel: 0933 652155

PHIL'S BRITISH BIKE BITS
204 Wellingborough Road
Rushden
Northamptonshire
NN10 9SX
Tel: 0933 53243

R.J. MOTORCYCLES
18-20 Hotel Street
Coalville
Leicestershire LE67 3EP
Tel: 0530 833297

ROAD STAR CYCLES
Victoria Park Mews
Dover
Kent CT16 1QS
Tel: 0304 202881

ROBERTSBRIDGE CLASSIC
MOTORCYCLES
Western House
Station Road
Robertsbridge
E. Sussex TN32 5DE
Tel: 0580 880323

SLATER LAVERDA
Collingtun, (Nr) Bromyard
Herefordshire HR7 4NB
Tel: 0885 410295

SUPREME CLASSICS
1 High Street
Earl Shilton
Leicestershire
Tel: 0455 841133

SURREY HARLEY-DAVIDSON
Unit 4/5 Havenbury Estate
Station Road
Dorking
Surrey RH4 1ES
Tel: 0306 883825

THUNDERBIRD CLASSICS
71 Church Street
Horwich
Bolton BL6 6AA
Tel: 0204 697275

T.M.S.
92-94 Carlton Road
Nottingham N93 2AS
Tel: 0602 503447

WILEMANS MOTORS
Siddals Road
Derby DE1 2P2
Tel: 0332 342813

Metal Polishing, Powder Coating, Chroming & Paints

CUSTOM PAINTWORK
The Roadhouse
Troydale Garage
Troydale Lane
Pudsey
W. Yorks LS28 9LD
Tel: 0532 559682

DREAM MACHINE
Unit 3
Derwent Street
Witsthorpe Road
Longeaton
Nottingham NG10 35W
Tel: 0602 736615

F.N.D. POLISHING CO.
Unit 13
Northcote Road
Bilston
Wolverhampton WV14 0PT
Tel: 0902 498855

J.P.C.
Unit 7
Orchard Road
Royston
Hertforshire SG8 5HA
Tel: 0763 241120

KINGSLEY CHROME
Unit 6
Kingsley Business Park
Kingsley
Hampshire GU35 9LY
Tel: 0420 489 676

KOLOUR SHOP
MOTORCYCLE PAINTWORK
SPECIALISTS
110 Langley Avenue West
Sheffield S5 8WF
Tel: 0742 425670

LONG EATON ENAMELLERS
Acton Avenue
Long Eaton
Nottingham NG10 1GA
Tel: 0602 723676

POWDER COATINGS LTD
Freepost BM2298
Birmingham B24 8NB
Tel: 021 328 4086

R.D. COX & SON
Phoenix Works
Phoenix Terrace
Harley Wintney
Hampshire RG27 8RY
Tel: 0252 845352

SCREENCRAFT LTD
17 Lombard Road
Wimbledon SW19 3TZ
Tel: 081 543 8977

SPORTS & VINTAGE
MOTORCYCLES LTD
Upper Battlefield
Shrewsbury SY4 3DB
Tel: 0939 210644

TRIPLE 'S' ENAMELLERS
Unit R6
Castlefield Industrial Estate
Bingley
West Yorkshire BD16 2AG
Tel: 0274 562474

VEHICLE, GENERAL POLISHERS &
PLATERS
Unit 1
Fairfield Industrial Estate
Arlesey
Bedfordshire SG15 6SR
Tel: 0462 730396

Publications

Classic Bike /Custom Bike
The Classic Motorcycle
EMAP National Publications Ltd
Bushfield House
Orton Centre
Peterborough
Cambridgeshire PE2 0UW
Tel: 0733 237111

Classic American
Motorcycle
The Classic Bike Guide
Myatt McFarlane Plc
PO Box 666
Altrincham
Cheshire WA15 2UD
Tel: 061 928 3480

Classic and Motorcycle
Mechanics
Classic Racer
Bob Berry Publishing
Services
Suite C/Deene House
Market Square
Corby
Northamptonshire NN17 1PB
Tel: 0536 203003

Motor Cycle News
'The Annexe'
Abbotts Court
34 Faringdon Lane
London EC1 3AU
Tel: 071 837 3699

The Vintage Motorcycle
Dalton Watson
c/o De Verdun Avenue
Belton
Loughborough
Leicestershire LE12 9TY
Tel: 0530 223569

Clubs

BRITISH MOTORCYCLE
OWNERS
P. Doggett
2 Thelnetham Road
Blo Norton
Norfolk IP22 2JQ (SAE)

BRITISH MOTORCYCLE
OWNERS
P. Coventry
59 Mackenzie Street
Bolton BL1 6QP

BRITISH MOTORCYCLISTS
FEDERATION
Jack Wiley House
129 Seaforth Avenue
Motspur Park
New Malden
Surrey KT3 6JM

BSA OWNERS CLUB
R. Jones
44 Froxfield Road
West Leigh
Havant
Hampshire PO9 5PW

DUCATI OWNERS CLUB
Membership Secretary:
Shirley Cottage
Reigate Road
Buckland
Reigate
Surrey RH2 9RE

HONDA OWNERS CLUB
(UK)
D. Barton
18 Embley Close
Calmore
Southampton SO4 3QX
(SAE)

INDIAN MOTORCYCLE CLUB
(UK)
J. Chatterton
183 Buxton Road
Newton
Newmills
Stockport
Cheshire SK12 3LA

MOTO GUZZI CLUB (UK)
S. Howers
26 Northwood Gardens
Greenford
Middlesex (SAE)

NORTON OWNERS CLUB
(UK)
D. Fenner
Beeches
Durley Brook Road
Durley
Southampton SO3 2AR

SUZUKI OWNERS CLUB
T. Harris
62 Northumberland
Road
New Barnet
Hertfordshire ENJ 1EE

TRIUMPH OWNERS
MOTORCYCLE CLUB
General Secretary:
Mr. M. Mellish
4 Douglas Avenue
Harold Wood
Romford
Essex RM3 0UT (SAE)

VINTAGE JAPANESE
MOTORCYCLE CLUB
C. Gibson
PO Box 1038
Bristol BS99 1US

VINTAGE MOTORCYCLE CLUB
Mrs. A. Davey
Allen House
Wetmore Road
Burton-on-Trent
Staffordshire DE14 1SN

YAMAHA RIDERS CLUB
Mr. D. Galbraith
64 Hawthorns
Saltash
Cornwall PL12 4BB

Index